Bitcoin Box Set:

Bitcoin Basics & Bitcoin Trading and Investing

BENJAMIN TIDEAS

Copyright © 2015 Plaid Enterprises

All rights reserved.

ISBN: **1511986476**
ISBN-13: **978-1511986472**

CONTENTS

	Introduction	i
1	Volume I: Bitcoin Basics	1
2	What Is Bitcoin And How Does It Work	2
3	The History Of Bitcoin	6
4	Buying And Selling Bitcoins	8
5	Investing In Bitcoins	10
6	Mining Bitcoins	13
7	Staying Safe: Avoiding Scams And Fraud	17
8	Benefits And Downfalls Of Bitcoin	20
9	Conclusion	22
10	Volume II: Bitcoin Trading And Investing	23
11	Real Life Usage	24
12	How Bitcoin Works	26
13	Exchanges	27
14	How To Become A Player In The Bitcoin Market	28
15	Becoming A Bitcoin Trader	29
16	Risks And Rewards	35
17	Success (And Cautionary) Stories	39
18	Conclusion	42

INTRODUCTION

Nice work picking up this 2 volume box set that includes two of my best-selling books: "Bitcoin Basics: Buying, Selling, Creating and Investing Bitcoins – The Digital Currency of the Future" AND "Bitcoin Trading and Investing: A Complete Beginners Guide to Buying, Selling, Investing and Trading Bitcoins". Please remember to use the end of this book to grab free reports, another free book and other extras that supplement this box set!

VOLUME I: BITCOIN BASICS

This book contains proven steps and strategies for understanding and getting started using Bitcoins. It also contains tips on how to avoid possible pitfalls in case you decide to put some good money into it.

Bitcoin has created such a huge impact on people's economic perspectives in such a short time that it is worthwhile to educate yourself about possibly making an investment.

Thanks again for grabbing this book, I hope you enjoy it! Now, let's get to it!

WHAT IS BITCOIN AND HOW DOES IT WORK?

Bitcoin is the first ever peer-to-peer digital currency created to facilitate online payments without the need of coursing the transactions through a financial institution. It is an electronic cash system designed to be the medium of exchange in the burgeoning internet commerce. Bitcoin has no physical attributes because it is purely a digital currency. There are no minted tokens or printed paper money to represent its value. Instead, it is an encoded algorithm (a 'hash', or a string of data) that is encrypted to represent one unit of currency.

There is no central authority that regulates Bitcoin. Instead, it uses cryptography to manage its creation and its transfer from one user to another. Management of the various transactions is a collective effort of the network.

Bitcoin is virtual money and like all other currencies in the world has its own stored value. Its value, however, is not backed by gold or other precious commodities like the currencies of gold. It is more like fiat currency (similar to the U.S. Dollar) which the issuing government money declares as legal tender despite not being backed by its weight in gold or silver. As fiat currencies that have values derived from the holder's faith in the countries issuing them, Bitcoins also derive their values from the holders' faith in the global digital network that oversees it.

Like fiat currencies, Bitcoins become acceptable as payment for goods and services simply because people have confidence in the issuing authority, which, in this case, is the Bitcoin network populated by users who believe in it. The bottom-line - as a peer-to-peer currency, the real value of the Bitcoin depends on how much of it the seller will be willing to part with his goods or services and how much of it the buyer will be willing to pay.

Bitcoin is described best as a crypto-currency that is purely digital, totally peer-to-peer, uncontrolled and unregulated by any central authority, and cannot be controlled nor regulated by any government. This only exists in your computers, smartphones, and tablets yet this still has the same buying power and value as any other currency.

How the Bitcoin System Works (For the Geeks)

Bitcoin is an electronic cash system that is dependent on and makes use of three essential elements to manage its creation and process and verify its every use. The vital elements are peer-to-peer networking, public key cryptography, and proof of work.

Peer-to-peer networking means it has no central authority to manage the operations and the responsibility of processing data and transactions shared by everyone connected to the network. Public key cryptography indicates it uses two different keys – a private key which is used to create a digital signature, and a public key which is used to verify the digital signature. Proof of work is a system used to prevent denial of service attacks – it comes in the form of a string of data that is difficult and tough to produce but once produced, affirms that the work was done.

Bitcoin circulation is fixed at 21,000,000 total digital coins which will be embedded (distributed) into the Bitcoin network nodes in batches with the number of coins to be cut in half every four years as follows: 10,500,000 – first; 5,250,000 – second; 2,625,000 – third; and so on. These coins will be released into the system through a process called 'mining' which will be discussed in detail, in another chapter of this book. To date, approximately 12,000,000 Bitcoins have been introduced into circulation since the first release on January 9, 2009.

They call the process of creating or retrieving the embedded Bitcoins 'mining' because, like miners, network users have to exert great effort to solve the difficult mathematical problems and create blocks before they are rewarded with the release of the new Bitcoins from the network nodes. Anyone can 'mine' for Bitcoins by using a free application called 'Bitcoin Miner' which can be downloaded for free from the Bitcoin website.

Every new Bitcoin introduced into the network originally comes from mining and given as a form of reward for block solutions to successful miners. Mining is solving a block of Bitcoin transactions by looking for a hash or a string of values that fits the network's stringent cryptographic rules. It is like solving a cryptographic puzzle. It may require several attempts before you are able to solve a block. Also, the level of difficulty increases as more of the Bitcoins go into circulation.

The Bitcoin 'miners' are essentially taking part in a collective effort designed to create a distributed consensus to confirm every Bitcoin transaction. In exchange for their efforts, miners are rewarded with new Bitcoins (at the time of this writing: 25 coins per block of transactions successfully processed or solved).

This is pretty much how the embedded Bitcoins are dug up, created, or generated and introduced into the system for the first time. After that, every time a Bitcoin changes hands, its digital signature is invalidated, and a new digital signature is assigned which in effect, destroys the old coin and creates a new one in the same place.

How the Bitcoin System Works (For the Less Geeky)

Even without understanding the technical details surrounding Bitcoin, a user can just as easily start using it simply by downloading and installing his own Bitcoin wallet on his desktop or any mobile device. Installing the Bitcoin wallet software will generate an address for you and you can create as many wallets as you want. You can now store the Bitcoins you purchased or received as payments in your wallet. To receive payment, you simply share your Bitcoin address with your friends or clients, and they can send their payments to this address, which is pretty much like sending email. It is as simple as that.

If you intend to install a Bitcoin wallet on your desktop, you can download the Multibit installer online. If you want to install a wallet on your smart phone or other mobile devices, then you can also download the Bitcoin Wallet installer for androids.

Where can you Use Bitcoins?

With Bitcoins stashed in your wallet, all you need now is to find vendors who'll accept them as payment. Like any other commodity, Bitcoins can be exchanged, bought, or sold. They can be used to buy goods or procure services from a growing number of shops that directly accept them, and they are spread out all across the globe and used by online shops as well as brick and mortar stores. You can buy anything from pizza to clothing, to electronic gadgets, etc. using Bitcoins today. Or you can simply exchange them for cash. You can also make use of related services such as Bitspend or Bitpay to purchase from the biggest online stores to the smallest online stores.

THE HISTORY OF BITCOIN

The idea of creating a digital currency came about for the first time in 1992 after a group of scientists headed by retired Intel physicist, Timothy May, met to discuss the issue of privacy and the then infantile internet which various governments around the world wanted to rein in. Specifically, the government wanted to prevent the use of cryptographic protocols that ensure privacy on the internet. The group called itself the Cypherpunks.

A lot of ideas on how to keep the internet private, independent and free from government regulatory measures were floated around. One of them, Jim Bell, floated the idea of creating a digital coin, but it was for a purpose totally unrelated to privacy issues. It was to solicit donations to fund assassination plots against government officials who go against the will of the people and set up an anarchic end which most in the group did not approve of.

Another cypherpunk member, a computer scientist by the name of Nick Szabo, proposed the creation of bit-gold, a digital currency which shall be free from intervention by any central authority and to be created from the ground up. He wanted bit-gold to serve as an alternative to the mainstream currencies.

It was Szabo who first floated the idea of encouraging users to solve puzzles and to reward those who can come up with solutions with the digital coins. In his Bitgold proposal, users will be encouraged to compete against each other to solve a string of challenge bits using the proof of work function (also known as secure benchmark functions). Unfortunately, his idea found no fruition since it encountered a lot of technical difficulties.

In 1998, at about the same time Szabo's Bitgold proposal was published, another cypherpunk, Wei Dai, a fresh graduate from the University of Washington published yet another proposal for creating B-money, a cryptocurrency that in essence was a distributed electronic cash system.

Unfortunately, both Nick Szabo's Bitgold and Wei Dai's B-money failed to generate support and could not get off the ground. Nothing about a digital currency was ever heard of for the next ten years. And when people were starting to think that the idea of an alternative digital currency have all but fizzled out, an email from a Satoshi Nakamoto containing a paper entitled "Bitcoin: A Peer-to-Peer Electronic Cash System" was sent to a cryptography mailing list on November 1, 2008, which had everyone talking. The discussion thread from this email grew extremely fast and included prominent figures in the mailing list such as Hal Finney.

Barely three months after this email, on January 9, 2009, Nakamoto released Bitcoin v0.1 to the same mailing list officially launching Bitcoin. On January 12, 2009, the first Bitcoin transaction was made involving 50 coins sent by Nakamoto to Hal Finney. On October 5, 2009, the first rate of exchange between Bitcoin and the USD was published by New Liberty Standard, which was pegged at $1 = 1,309.03 Bitcoins.

Bitcoins started with the value of mere pennies but quickly rose after that. The value rose in popularity as more and more entities began accepting it. In 2011, it hit the peak of $32 to buy one Bitcoin rising from the mere $0.30 value it had at the start. It amazingly hit a high of $1230 momentarily in 2012 and has settled at an average of $235.00 today. Occasionally, speculators have shown great interest and entered the fray pushing the price of a Bitcoin to record highs in the Bitcoin exchanges. At current writing, it is trading around $250.

BUYING AND SELLING BITCOINS

You need to have a Bitcoin wallet first before you can buy or sell Bitcoins. The Bitcoin wallet is where the coins are received and sent, without which a transaction won't push through. Creating a Bitcoin wallet is easy. All you need to do is download a Bitcoin client application and run it.

There are 3 types of Bitcoin wallet applications available:

Some of the more popular software wallets include Multibit, Blockchain.info, Bitcoin Core, and Armory. Software wallets are those that you install on desktops. With software wallets, you maintain complete control and responsibility of your money including protecting it from being hacked and creating backup files.

Mobile wallets such as the Bitcoin Wallet for Android, for example, are available on Google Play. Mobile wallets are installed on your mobile device or smartphones. This means you can bring your Bitcoins everywhere you go and use them at any brick and mortar stores that accept Bitcoins. To pay using your mobile wallet, you would simply scan the QR code or use the NFC 'tap to pay' application.

Online wallets are hosted Bitcoin wallets, the most popular being Coinbase. You'd be able to use them anywhere that there is internet access. However, since third party hosting services will keep your bitcoins, you need to be extra careful in choosing the most trustworthy among them.

You can download the Multibit installer online for free if you are installing your wallet on a desktop. If you want to install a wallet on your smart phone or other mobile devices, then you can download the Bitcoin Wallet installer for androids at Google Play.

With a Bitcoin wallet, you can now start acquiring and transacting Bitcoins. You can now accept them as payment for the goods or services you offer if you are into some kind of business. If you want to obtain more Bitcoins, you can go to any of the existing Bitcoin Exchanges. But, of course, the easiest way to obtain Bitcoins is to buy them from someone you know who has them. Or, you can also get them for free as offers or bonuses from some online shops and gaming applications as an incentive for your purchase and/or patronage.

Please note that Bitcoin exchanges do not accept credit card or PayPal payments. This is because they can easily arbitrarily reverse payments which will leave the Bitcoins in the hands of the buyer, who can surreptitiously get his money back via a chargeback by filing a concocted complaint. It may be possible to find people who will sell Bitcoins in exchange for a credit card or PayPal payment, but your best bet is to buy from the exchange and pay instead via money transfer services.

INVESTING IN BITCOINS

The Bitcoin economy may still be in its infancy stage, but the value of the Bitcoins in circulation today is roughly estimated at around $2 billion and continues to rise rapidly. On top of that, budding services that will beef up the Bitcoin economy are sprouting like mushrooms all over the world. It will be hard not to notice a growing number of techno-geeks who dedicate their time, money, and skills to developing digital wallet applications, creating Bitcoin payment processors, building Bitcoin exchanges - all in support of establishing a robust Bitcoin ecosystem.

Inescapable too is the increasing number of establishments from every corner of the globe, online or otherwise, that are now accepting Bitcoins alongside the US Dollar, the Euro, and the Yen as payment for traditional goods and services. With people growing wary of the high fees being charged on credit card transactions, and their developing distrust for the banking institution all over the world in the heels of the JP Morgan debacle and other scandals involving prominent financial institutions, Bitcoin just may be viewed as the best safe haven for valuable capital, next to gold.

The Huge Potential of Bitcoin

Financial experts agree that the potential for growth of Bitcoin is huge and unfathomable as of this time. Some of them even believe it can replace gold calling it Gold 2.0. Compared to gold, this crypto-currency is easy to use for any transaction, and it will cost you nothing to store it, not to mention the fact that it is free from the regulatory manipulations of any government or central authority.

When it was first introduced in 2009, Bitcoin costs only $0.30 each. As of this writing, it's trading above $250, briefly touching the $400 level, and still poised for more upward vertical movement. But the question in everybody's mind is how far up it can go?

Believe it or not but there are financial experts who pegged the value of Bitcoin at $400,000 each! And if you are wondering how they came up with this seemingly scandalous figure, well, it came up with the assumption that Bitcoin will in due time replace gold. By extrapolating the current value of all the gold in the world ($8 trillion) to the total number of Bitcoins (21,000,000) that will be in circulation, you'll come up with $400,000 ($8 trillion divided by 21,000,000 Bitcoins. This serves as the upper limits of the potential value of Bitcoins, and that is just for starters. Who knows how much more it can appreciate in value if some countries start using it as their reserve currency, which incidentally is not too far-fetched.

But, hold your horses! Before you take the plunge and place all your investible funds into Bitcoins, you must consider the fact that this is an emerging technology, and it would be inadvisable to throw caution to the wind. The more experienced investors who believe there are bright prospects for this virtual currency in the future are timidly placing their investments in it, limiting their exposure to Bitcoins to no more than 1% of their portfolio. You should too. It would be disastrous to consider investing on Bitcoins as a get-rich-quick scheme.

So, how do you invest in Bitcoins?

Buying and selling Bitcoins is easy. There are a number of Bitcoin exchanges where you can buy or sell Bitcoins much like the stock market where buy orders are matched with existing sell orders. The prices of Bitcoins are quoted on real time basis depending on the latest price it is currently trading.

If you want a more stable pricing plan, you can go to a fixed rate Bitcoin broker instead. These are the small Bitcoin buy and sell merchants who make money by putting a small spread between buying and selling prices.

Then there are bulk Bitcoin buyers who only buy and sell the coins in amounts of $10,000 or higher. They are the liquidity providers in the Bitcoin investment landscape.

Don't blink now but there are also physical Bitcoins you can buy. Physical Bitcoins are actual bearer tokens with an embedded Bitcoin value that can only be redeemed if the coin is torn open. This is one of the easiest ways to accumulate Bitcoins because you can use PayPal or even your credit card to purchase these coins.

However, whichever way you chose to acquire Bitcoins, it is necessary to exert extra effort to determine the real world identity of the dealers or the operators of the exchange before sending your money to any of them. Trading in Bitcoins is highly unregulated, and there is a high risk you may end up dealing with an unscrupulous operator who will abscond with your money.

It is best to visit their websites and get to know the people behind the company first. You can also browse various Bitcoin forums with an eye for any negative feedback from previous users of the Bitcoin exchanges with whom you are considering transacting.

MINING BITCOINS

The best way to understand is to compare it to gold. Gold is rare or in limited supply, and it derives its value from the fact that people want it. Like gold, the supply of Bitcoin is limited (capped at 21,000,000 coins). It also has value because people give them value for numerous reasons.

The most important analogy is that gold is produced by mining them and similarly Bitcoins are produced through a process called mining. The only difference while you dig dirt for the gold, with Bitcoin, the mining is purely a mathematical process.

A total of 21,000,000 Bitcoins have been distributed (or embedded) in the Bitcoin network nodes. In order to 'dig up' the Bitcoins, participants (called miners) will have to pack a group of Bitcoin transactions into a block and then search for a string of data that matches a particular pattern when the Bitcoin cryptographic hash is applied to it. Whoever is first to make a match for a particular block unlocks a bunch of Bitcoins (currently at 25) as his reward or bounty. The bounty becomes smaller while the level of difficulty increases as more and more of the Bitcoins are unlocked. It can be likened to looking for prime numbers where it will be easy to find the smaller primes but becomes exceedingly difficult as you progress into the larger numbers.

Here is the sequence of events for Bitcoin mining:

1. When new Bitcoin transactions occur, they are promptly transmitted to all the Bitcoin network nodes.
2. A miner collects new transactions that enter his node and packs them into a block.

3. He then starts searching for that matching string of data that will be the proof-of-work for his block.
4. When a miner discovers a proof-of-work, the solved block is immediately broadcasted to all the other nodes in the network.
5. New Bitcoins are then released to the node of the miner who found the proof-of-work first.
6. The system as a whole accepts the block only after the majority of the nodes agree that all transactions in it are valid, and none of the Bitcoins involved have already been spent.
7. Acceptance of the block is confirmed by the creation of the next block in the chain where the algorithm value of the accepted block becomes the hash of the previous block.

As you may have noticed, the Bitcoin 'miners' are essentially taking part in a collective effort designed to generate a distributed consensus to confirm every Bitcoin transaction. At the same time, they strengthen the integrity of the network as well as ensure that everybody is synchronized with one another.

To Mine or not to Mine

Mining requires a great deal of computing power to process the increasing number of transactions. Much more so because the level of difficulty has increased to the point that it now requires billions of calculations per second to produce a single proof of work. On top of that, more miners are joining the fray. Many of them are equipped with more powerful GPUs (Graphics Processing Units) or gaming computers that are a thousand times more powerful than the regular CPUs.

Others have even built supercomputers dedicated to Bitcoin mining using the ASICs (Application Specific Integrated Circuits), which is the same technology used in modern cell phones and other mobile devices. Mining Bitcoins all by your lonesome self, using a regular computer will only make you eat the dust of the most sophisticated miners. It will take you ages to be able to solve a block. Remember, it is a game of who gets to solve a block first.

Your best bet if you want to go Bitcoin mining at this point in time is to join mining pools. A mining pool combines the computing power of a group of miners with the work divided among them. Everyone gets a share of the bounty from every solved block commensurate to the amount of work he has contributed.

The only problem with pool mining is the possibility of the pool operator absconding with your Bitcoin bounty and keeping them for himself. While this is something that can't be discounted, the risk can be minimized by making a careful choice. It is best that before joining any mining pool, you should scan the various Bitcoin mining forums to look for mining pools with positive feedbacks and stay away from those with unacceptable comments.

There are now Cloud Mining sites that will, in essence, rent you the computational power required to mine bitcoins. Since it is quite difficult to harness the required amount of power to mine on one's own. Instead of adding your machine to the pool, you rent someone else's anonymous machine to do the mining for you. It is easier than it sounds, and probably the most realistic way to get into Bitcoin mining for the first time.

To get you started here is a list of top Bitcoin Mining Pools (with Links!) you may consider researching/joining:

• CEX.IO - For Cloud Mining, you actually purchase GHS, or Bitcoin cloud mining power, according to market price, and your GHS will start mining for you immediately. With CEX.IO, you can sell your GHS at any time, or even trade them for fiat money or crypto-currencies and make a profit.
• BTC Guild - BTC Guild is one of the pioneering Bitcoin Mining Pools, which still operates as of writing and tops everyone else, accounting for 30% of the total blocks found for 2013. It provides a simple but feature-filled interface for its users.
• Slush Pool- aka MiningBitcoinCZ – accounts for 10% of the total blocks found in 2013. It was the first mining pool created and has been in operation since December, 2010. It boasts of having a consistent and stable payout since the start of its operations.
• Bit minter – accounts for 5% of total blocks found for 2013. It boasts of having an innovative, gauge metered mining software which runs with just one click.
• Eclipse – accounts for 4% of total blocks found for 2013.
• Asic Miner – accounts for 4% of total blocks found for 2013.This is a mining company where instead of mining yourself you buy shares of the company, and you make money through dividend earnings.
• Ozcoin – accounts for 4% of total blocks found for 2013. Features Double Geometric Payout with only 1% transaction fee.

For more mining pool listings and comparative studies, you may browse the web. If you want to know the most current developments in the Bitcoin economic landscape, you may also join online forums that discuss Bitcoins. CoinDesk usually has informative, relevant, unbiased articles. This will enable you to read even more of what everyone is talking about.

STAYING SAFE: AVOIDING SCAMS AND FRAUD

Bitcoin exists in the virtual world populated not only by caring and responsible 'netizens' who found a niche for themselves there, but also by tech savvy bigots out to disrupt the order and serenity of the flourishing virtual realm. They look for vulnerabilities to breach security protocols and deface websites. They steal your identities and use your credit card to make purchases for themselves, leaving your credit history in a shambles. They hack financial institutions and rob them of their money to enrich themselves. Worst, they do all these just to prove they are a breed apart from the rest of the internet citizenry, and that they are the lords and masters of the virtual realm.

It will be wishful thinking to expect that they will spare Bitcoin from their attacks. Fortunately, the Bitcoin system is so well designed that there never have been any major disruption which hindered its operation from the time the system was birthed in 2009. Of course, there are no perfect systems and hackers are always out there to prove this. Admittedly, there were security flaws and vulnerabilities in the Bitcoin system but they were always discovered early and corrected before hackers could exploit them.

As the largest distributed computing project on the internet, you would usually expect Bitcoin to have plenty of such weaknesses and be an easy target for hackers. Fortunately, Bitcoin's well-designed protocol and cryptography has made it almost impossible for hackers to shut down the system. It has, in fact, stood the test of time as is evident from its unblemished security track record.

Nevertheless, there is a continuous stream of reports citing massive losses of Bitcoins. In most instances, however, the losses are mainly due to the negligence of the users usually involving cases where the Bitcoin wallet files were lost, accidentally deleted, or hacked. Mounting reports of massive Bitcoin losses have also been noted, all of which have been attributed to hackers, scammers, and fraudsters.

Attacks on Bitcoin exchanges and other Bitcoin businesses have been on the rise lately - no thanks to the surging value of the crypto-currency in the market. Such incidents have become rampant, more frequent, and worrisome.

Bitcoin exchanges and other Bitcoin businesses have become fair game to hackers because they use third party Bitcoin software and other proprietary applications developed independently to promote Bitcoin trade with their services. And, like all other software, these proprietary client applications have inherent vulnerabilities that hackers love to discover and exploit.

If we are to gauge it by the increasing number of incident reports related to Bitcoin losses, it seems that the digital marauders are having a field day hacking Bitcoin wallets, dry feasting on the Bitcoin exchanges (which have become their favorite targets) and other Bitcoin businesses.

Like the hackers, the scammers and fraudsters are also having a field day capitalizing on the growing popularity of the crypto-currency by duping unsuspecting 'netizens' and robbing them of their hard-earned cash and Bitcoins. They establish fake Bitcoin exchanges or set up online businesses that accept Bitcoins for payments only to close shop promptly the minute someone starts questioning their legitimacy. They accept payments and/or deposits in Bitcoins and cash without delivering the promised goods or services.

Because of all these unfortunate incidents, a large cloud of doubt has fallen over Bitcoin as people have started developing negative notions about the Bitcoin ecosystem and on the integrity and safety of investing in it. The bottom line is none of these unfortunate incidents point to any vulnerability in the Bitcoin system itself. Its security protocols have remained intact and strong. And, notwithstanding the constant attacks from hackers, scammers, and fraudsters, the Bitcoin economy continues to flourish. The demand is rising and its rate doubling in value at an unbelievable pace.

As of current writing, a lot of investors want a slice of the Bitcoin pie, but they are being held back by such questions as - how can they stay safe in the face of the seemingly relentless hacking attacks? How can they protect themselves from being scammed and defrauded of their hard earned cash and Bitcoins?

There is only one answer to this – eternal vigilance. You need to actively participate in the various Bitcoin forums where you will get to know which company to deal and what Bitcoin services to use. It is in the forums where you will learn who not to deal with and which exchanges to avoid.

Here are some helpful tips on how you can stay safe and avoid being robbed or scammed:

- If you have a stash of Bitcoins in your possession, do not make the mistake of putting all of them in one place. Create at least two wallets (more if you have stashed quite a bit of fortune) – one wallet shall serve as your everyday wallet. This is what you will use for your day to day Bitcoin transactions, which means it will be available most of the time. Make sure you keep the amount of Bitcoins in this wallet to a minimum. The other wallet(s) will serve as your vault or depository. This is where you will receive Bitcoin payments. You need to keep this wallet in a detachable drive like a USB stick and keep it somewhere safe. You should only access it or put it online only when it is necessary. Remember, hackers will only be able to hack wallets if they are stored in computers that are online. If the wallet is not accessible online, hackers won't be able to reach it and empty its contents. Don't worry because you can continue to add coins to it even if it is kept hidden somewhere safe, completely detached from your computer. All you need is to declare the network address of this wallet and people can send Bitcoins to it. In short, it will continue to accumulate Bitcoins even if it is kept out of reach of the prying eyes of scammers.
- Always back up your Bitcoin wallet files and keep your backup files somewhere safe too. This way, you'd be able to recover the data if you accidentally erase your files or if your computer gets infected by a virus.
- Don't be tempted to use cloud services to store your Bitcoins. They are fair game and a favorite target of scammers nowadays.

Before dealing with an exchange or another Bitcoin business entity, you must do some due diligence work first. Get to know who the people are behind the company. Better still; get the physical address of the business if you can. Never deal with a company whose owners remain incognito. This way, you will have recourse if things turn sour.

BENEFITS AND DOWNFALLS OF BITCOIN

Everyone appears to have been bitten by the Bitcoin bug. The internet is buzzing with news and updates about it, and you'd be hard pressed to read an entire newspaper or financial magazine without stumbling on an article discussing its merits. More significant is the steady flow of precious capital from young entrepreneurs to fund Bitcoin start-ups.

Most notable among them is the $5 million investment made by Fred Wilson of Union Square Ventures to fund Coinbase, a startup that converts US dollars into Bitcoins and vice versa for a 1%transaction fee. (Union Square Ventures is a venture capital firm which invests on IT startups with high potentials for growth.)

Do you remember the Winklevoss twins of the Facebook fame (who claimed that Facebook was their original idea and not Zuckerberg's)? They too poured in $11 million hard currency to purchase Bitcoins, which left everybody's mouth gaping in amazement and wondering what is it they saw in Bitcoin that made them make such a determined move.

Here is what these young entrepreneurs saw – the benefits that can be derived from the crypto-currency:

• Untraceable transactions – Bitcoins can be sent peer to peer in total anonymity. Bitcoins are sent from one network address to another without anyone knowing whose addresses they are.
• Gives users full control – anyone can send or receive money anytime and anywhere in the world without limits and without the need of coursing it through a bank or any other financial intermediary.
• The risk of inflation is low – Unlike most fiat currencies that can be printed at will and in volumes dictated by the issuing government, the

quantity of Bitcoins that will be in circulation is fixed at no more and no less than 21,000,000, which means its purchasing power will be more stable.

• Very low or no transaction fees – Bitcoin transactions are processed with low or no transaction fees which makes it a superior choice because it will cost less to make payments compared to using credit cards, PayPal, or other online payment platforms.

• Secure payments, a lower risk for merchants - With Bitcoins, merchants don't have to worry about fraudulent chargebacks like they do with a credit card or PayPal payments. Bitcoin transactions are also totally irreversible. Once the payment is made, that's it.

• It requires no PCI compilation – as is required of merchants accepting credit card payments, so it also allows merchants to do business even in places where credit cards are not available. On top of that, it is tax-free.

• Free from control or intervention by any central authority or government – With a cryptographically secure protocol, Bitcoin cannot be controlled or manipulated by anyone or any entity. It is also transparent with all the information about it embedded in the block chain. It is neutral allowing everyone to view, verify, and use it anytime in real time.

• Can be carried anywhere – You can bring along a million dollars worth of Bitcoins with you inconspicuously because they will easily fit onto a memory stick. This is something you can't do with hard cash or gold.

There are always two sides to a coin (pun slightly intended), which means if there are benefits, there must be some downfalls too. For Bitcoin, the downfalls are as follows:

• Limited Acceptance (at least currently) – The list of commercial establishments that directly accepts Bitcoin payments is still small although it is growing at a steady rate. The limited number of Bitcoin establishments dissuades many consumers from dipping into it, which can slow its growth.

• Untraceable – This is both a benefit and a disadvantage. People love it because they can send payments without it being traced back to them. This means, in the hands of shady individuals, it provides them the opportunity to purchase drugs or fund illicit trade without it being traced back to them.

• Highly Volatile – with a limited number of Bitcoins in circulation today faced by an increasing demand for it, the value of Bitcoins can fluctuate like crazy, fueled by even the smallest event or the weirdest market development.

Competing Crypto Currencies – Bitcoin may be the only virtual currency for now that has attained an acceptable level of success, but there is always a possibility that other crypto-currencies may pop out in the future and become more successful than Bitcoin.

CONCLUSION

I sincerely hope the information contained will help you to understand the basics of the digital currency of the future: Bitcoins. In an ever-evolving global economy, it's easy to see the benefits of this crypto-currency while also recognizing the possible pitfalls. The best idea is to keep yourself abreast of the information and staying well-informed of the technology and logistics behind this game-changing digital currency of the future.

The next step is to put into practice the knowledge and employ the strategies we've discussed here to begin making Bitcoins work for you and your future!

Get Your FREE Cryptocurrencies Cheat Sheet and 5-day Mini-Course HERE!

www.plaid-enterprises.com/bitcoin

VOLUME II: BITCOIN TRADING AND INVESTING

I want to congratulate you and thank you for picking up this book, "Bitcoin Trading and Investing: A Complete Beginners Guide to Buying, Selling, Investing, and Trading Bitcoins".

The digital rush sweeping the globe, and, in particular, the internet, has centered around investors of all ages and lifestyles cashing in on Bitcoin. It's the infamously unpredictable cryptocurrency that makes trading and investing as easy as sitting in front of your laptop. However, what is easy is not always simple. Part of the reason it is difficult to grasp is because it has not been around for long – there is no way to truthfully psychoanalyze the comings and goings, the rises and the falls of what your currency can do. Getting involved with Bitcoin is easier and riskier than the traditional ways we think about investments. However, just like with Wall Street, there are ways to become more proficient in the art of trading and investing.

As with any exchange, market, or online platform that requires a credit card, trading with Bitcoin is risky to those who are new, and those who have been working at it for quite some time. Though you probably will never hold Bitcoins in your hands, it can hurt your bottom line – you might lose real money. The most important advice you can receive is to proceed with caution and make sure you are not pushing yourself deep into a hole.

This book will try to educate you on the options you have when it comes to trading and investing with Bitcoin. Read thoroughly before you try to start the process, make notes, and maybe sit by a prospect what is going on before you venture out on your own.

Thanks again for picking up this book, I hope you enjoy it! Now, let's get started!

REAL LIFE USAGE

With the emergence of Bitcoins as a major currency, there has been a need to use them in daily life, not just on the computer. While this is still emerging technology, there are a few ways to use Bitcoins to make purchases at stores, online, and for events.

Bitcoin ATMs

A Bitcoin ATM is an electronic communications device that allows a person to exchange bitcoins for cash without being connected to the internet or his or her wallet. There are two chief types of Bitcoin ATMs available in certain sections of the population. The basic units, which are more prevalent, allow the customer to only buy Bitcoins. The more complex machines, which are emerging but not as prevalent, will let a person buy as well as sell bitcoins via the machine. It's a completely revolutionary way for people to stay on top of their trading while they are on vacation, on business, or just away from computer access. There is one catch, however. In order to be able to access the more advanced and premium features of the complex units, you will usually need to be a member of the ATM manufacturer that operates the machine.

The first Bitcoin ATM was a Robocoin in a coffee shop in Canada. Soon the United States caught on. Most Bitcoin ATMs are located inside of independently owned coffee shops. There are currently 285 Bitcoin ATM Machines installed worldwide, but that number is always fluctuating.

In order to find a Bitcoin ATM, users can check the following websites:

- CoinATMRadar.com
- BitcoinATMmap.com

- Bitcoin ATM Locator by Forexmex.com

There is one problem: the more Bitcoin ATMs there are, the more, it seems hackers seem to target them.

Retailers Accepting Bitcoins

There are many different websites and retailers that accept Bitcoins as payment. Some even offer specials or discounts to those who use them. Here are some as of this writing:

- Microsoft – use on Windows, Windows phones, and Xbox
- Dell – Accepts Bitcoin through a partnership with Coinbase. Sometimes there are specials for users. Dell is the biggest acceptor of Bitcoins.
- Overstock – One of the first major retailers to accept the currency. Bitcoin purchases are open to over 100 countries.
- Newegg – A retail giant based in Los Angeles, CA. It specializes in computer hardware and software, but also sells a variety of appliances and goods.
- Show Room Prive – The largest European Company to accept the payment via the company Paymium. Is not valid on the mobile platform.
- TigerDirect - the online retailer of computers and consumer electronics now accepts payments in Bitcoin,
- Bitcoinshop.us - Offers products from air-conditioners to watches, all priced in Bitcoin for those wanting to make a purchase. The catch: it only ships to people in the continental US.
- BitcoinStore.com - Sells electronics and ships worldwide.

The good news for those who don't like to make purchases on the internet is that there are hundreds of small retailers accepting bitcoin too. Coinmap, Spendbitcoins.com, and UseBitcoins.info keep up-to-date databases of these shopping destinations.

HOW BITCOIN WORKS

Though we've gone further in depth with this in a previous book, let us first start with a brief description of what Bitcoin is, and how it functions as a currency. The first step in trading Bitcoins is really understanding what they are, where they come from, and how to acquire more. Bitcoin is just like any other form of money though it is digital. As with other real forms of money, it can be saved, spent, invested, and even stolen through no fault of your own. What began as a small online forum in 2009 by someone using the name Satoshi Nakamoto, has grown in value and prestige in just a few short years. The value of the "dollar" or coin has also jumped significantly.

One generates Bitcoins through a process called "mining." Without going into too much detail, this is essentially using your computer's processor to solve complex algorithms known as "blocks." You will earn about fifty Bitcoins per block you have decrypted. There is a fairly large catch, depending on your computer and CPU, solving a single block can take you over a year. Another way to put Bitcoins into your virtual wallet is to simply purchase them using another form of money – you exchange it at a Bitcoin exchange station like Coin.mx, coinbase, or Bitstamp. There are many services all over the internet and they pop up randomly all of the time. The most important thing to do is to make sure they are reputable and trustworthy, usually by how long they've been around. Make sure you read testimonials and try to ensure that the website is not going to take your money.

EXCHANGES

Bitcoin exchanges happen just like physical currency exchanges do: you are purchasing one form of currency and trading it with another.

The relative value of whatever nation you are in is a reflection of the country's economy, financial health, and world status. For example, the U.S. dollar is worth more than that of the Mexican peso at the current time because of the differences between the economies. These values constantly fluctuate. The same type of thing happens with Bitcoins. The relative value is determined by the work performed by your individual computer. This also opens up a pathway that allows Bitcoins to be traded like commodities – just the way we trade eggs, playing cards, and secrets.

You make physical money by using previously mentioned websites as an intermediary for transactions between Bitcoins and national currencies. You watch the unpredictable shifts in relative values and simply trade back and forth. That's how some people make money – they simply shift money around when it is the proper moment. This is known as arbitrage, and it is probably the simplest form of trading available to Bitcoin users: but that also means many more people will lose money trying to navigate the twists and turns.

HOW TO BECOME A PLAYER IN THE BITCOIN MARKET

Knowing the risks and rewards, one can venture toward trading and invest in Bitcoins. There are quite a few different ways to go about making money for your trades. The best approach is to come up with a lump sum to keep yourself in line. You don't want to get too obsessed with "playing the market" or watching the rises and falls of the value.

Bitcoins are stored in a digital wallet that exists on your computer. Do not store large amounts of money in your Bitcoin wallet. Instead, keep them stored offline or in something known as "cold storage." Remember to keep your identity hidden when you are making a transaction - there's no need to identify yourself. Your comings and goings will be registered in a public log – but the buyer and seller of the goods are not revealed.

BECOMING A BITCOIN TRADER

There are several ways to dip your toes into the Bitcoin market and become a trader. Anyone can do it, and each entry point ranges from simple to difficult. Let's introduce a few of the ways to get wet in the Bitcoin trading market.

Bitcoin Mining

Mining is the easiest and slowest way into the market. Your best bet is to get a computer that will do nothing but mine for Bitcoins. You will have to install some software and just completely let the computer go – anything else you do causes you to lose money because you're pulling processing power away from mining. It is best to build your own computer that works extremely fast - some computers can take upwards of a year to actually see any profits. For this reason, mining has become a second thought to anyone who isn't sporting a full server center (yes, hundreds of boxes) with the newest, most powerful ASIC machines.

Mining Bitcoins is at a stage now where you probably won't make back your investment any time soon if you actually ever do. In truth, you are far more likely to see a greater profit margin if you go out and sell lemonade at the local pool during the summer. There are a few different things you can do, however, to make earning more Bitcoins easier and faster.

Trading Bots

Mt. Gox was one of the first to develop an automated trading bot, dubbed "Willy" to do some of the work for you. These bots, which aren't universally loved, trade on the financial markets so that users don't miss out on any potential sales. The question is – what exactly are these bots and can they really make money for you?

Trading bots are not humans, but are actually software programs that interact directly with financial exchanges, and place buy and sell orders on your behalf using artificial intelligence and algorithms. They make those decisions by watching the market's price movements and reacting according to a set of predefined rules. They aren't as good as humans are, of course, but they can let you sleep soundly.

Examples of other types of bots include the Butter Bot, which even features an online trading bot accessed via a Google Chrome plug-in, and Haas Online, which sells a Windows-based personal trading server. Another, Crypto Trader offers a trading bot marketplace, which allows people to develop bots using different trading strategies, and then rent them to others. This is the best chance to personalize a bot and make it work just like you would. Still, that takes a lot of effort and know-how.

Trading by algorithm isn't new in the financial world or even gambling, in general: companies in the conventional financial markets have been using the method for years. This empowers individual traders to have their computer access the exchange's electronic order books directly. That's a service normally only available to brokers and investment houses in the conventional markets. Once again, this isn't something that will take away the work for you, but will supplement what you already do. Pablo Lema, the founder of Butter Bot, says that bots aren't a 'fire and forget' technology that enable dilettantes to make money without trying:

"Trading bots require users to have at least a basic understanding of the market, need to be modified and tweaked by the user according to the predominant market conditions, and also according to their own risk profile."

Trading Bot Strategy

But of course you know that trading isn't necessarily based on technical analysis and algorithms alone. It's difficult to program a computer to react to fundamental market conditions such as, say, rumors about the market shut down or an upcoming news piece that will cause money to flood the market.

Many bots will use an exponential moving average (EMA) as a starting point. These averages act to track market prices over an established time span, and bots can be programmed to react to what that price does – such as moving beyond certain thresholds.

It's Not for Everyone

Is bot trading the solution for you? Possibly, but not definitely. They do offer a variety of rewards, not least of which is the ability to diligently trade on your behalf, 24/7, and the ability to remove all of the emotions from trading. Plus they allow you to "live and let live" – some people, especially newer traders, are too antsy with the clicking and make mistakes.

On the other hand, if you don't have the financial know-how to put together a trading strategy that will work for you and your bot, you could simply end up automating a set of poor market trading decisions.

Once again, whether or not you decide to automate your trades, the basic rules apply: don't trade more than you can afford to lose, and don't go into any investment without at least a basic understanding of what you're doing.

Finally, do yourself a favor and get a true assessment of what your risk tolerance really is. Many people think their tolerance is very high, but when they lose a large sum due to a market turn, they find quite abruptly that this is not so. Go here to find yours: Investment Risk Tolerance Quiz

Create a Gang

A "gang" or mining pool is an option. To use a mining pool, you have to find people to connect computers with so that you can all work together to break up the block. The money that comes from that block is then shared amongst the owners of the computers. However, it all depends on how much work your individual computer has put out – you won't get coins for just connecting and not putting in the work.

You can find pools all over the internet, just a simple Google search will amass millions of results. Bitcoin also has a large list of these popular mining gangs that you can join. The gangs for Bitcoin will give you a lot more information as to the team makeup, including where certain fees will go.

However, the level of security, if it is used at all, deviates from mining pool to mining pool. Some pools require only a Bitcoin trading username while others require the traditional two-step Google authentication process.

Still, Bitcoin remains as anonymous as ever, and you won't have to give out any personal information or numbers. This is a positive, as you are sometimes dealing with substantial amounts of money and sensitive information.

Head Straight for the Markets

Another approach you can take, though it is by far the riskiest move of all, is to jump right into the market and get to work. All you have to do is sign up with one of the companies listed above (Bitstamp, Coinbase, BTC-e and Cryptsy). Give them your email address, create a username, and confirm your account. It's fairly easy!

After you have confirmed your account, the website you chose will ask you to provide some forms that prove your identity, location, and tax status. These forms will most likely include any of the following:

- Any document issued by the or county, city, or the federal government;
- State of Residence Vehicle Registration Card or title;
- State of Residence Voter Precinct Card;
- Military Orders/Documents;
- Utility bill or cable bill;
- Housing lease or contract, mortgage statement, property or income tax statement;
- Preprinted financial statement;
- School records;
- State of Residence Vehicle insurance policy;
- Letter from the homeless shelter

You will also have to provide some form of identification that shows you have proof of a legal presence within the United States or country of your choice. These documents include:

- I-551 Permanent Resident Card
- Machine Readable Immigrant Visa
- I-766 Employment Authorization Card
- Temporary I-551 stamp on I-94 or Passport
- I-327 Re-entry Permit with supporting immigration documentation
- I-94 Arrival/Departure Record
- I-20 accompanied by I-94
- DS-2019 accompanied by I-94
- I-571 Refugee Travel Document with supporting immigration

documentation
- I-797 Notice of Action
- I-521L Authorization for Parole of an Alien into U.S. with supporting immigration documentation
- I-220B Order of supervision with supporting immigration documentation

Some web sites, though not all, will ask for proof for Social Security purposes. You will need to provide at least one of these documents:

- Social Security Card
- 1099 Tax Form
- W-2 Form
- DD-214 Form
- Payroll Record
- Social Security Document reflecting the Social Security Number
- Military Record reflecting the Social Security Number
- Medicaid/Medicare Card reflecting the Social Security Number

Most of these documents are things you'll have sitting around the house if you need them, so they shouldn't be too difficult to get. However, you will need to scan the documents in and send them to the company before you can start.

After you go through all of that, it is simply a matter of putting what you made into your account and watching the market on a daily or hourly basis for the opportunity to buy and sell to make more money. Some exchanges will charge a fee on any transaction you make, which will range from .25 per trade to .60 per trade. This is how these companies make money – because people know this has a chance to be the most successful venture for them.

Playing the markets requires you to be alert. You do stand a chance to lose some of your money through this method. In fact, it is probably the riskier option overall. You should only choose this method if you are willing to dedicate a large chunk of your time to this process. You can't only check the numbers once a week. Those who make the most money constantly pay attention to the rises and falls, and sell as soon as they know the time is right. If you don't have the time because you are working a lot or raising a family, you should consider another approach like a mining pool or mining by yourself.

Whichever way you choose to go: mining, joining a gang, or playing the market by yourself, there are risks and rewards associated with all of them. It really depends on what you want to get out of the entire process.

Mining takes longer, might not get you a profit, but is solitary and doesn't require you to work with people or constantly pay attention. However, it is very solitary and won't get you a lot of money.

Joining a mining pool is a somewhat more social experiment, but requires you to be at the mercy of other people and their computers, something that scares people away from doing that particular way of trading and making money.

Playing the market is the way to go for someone who wants to see instant action or results. However, it isn't for people who don't have income to lose. You will probably make mistakes for the first few months that you try to work with the market, and will keep doing so until you get a proper read for it.

RISKS AND REWARDS

Now that you know how to start your way into Bitcoin trading and investing, you should probably know the risks in detail. It's one thing to hear about the categories, but you also need to know what you are setting yourself up for. Most of these aren't problems, they are just things that will take you a little more time when you do your taxes or balance your checking account. Still, there are some risks and rewards you need to know about.

The Volatility of the Market

For most other forms of trading, including the stock market, the value of the currency rises and falls in a predictable way at a predictable speed. Rarely are there intense crashes in value or surges in costs. However, that is not the case with Bitcoin. The value of the Bitcoin falls and soars radically throughout the day, sometimes peaking the morning or peaking at night – there is rarely a rhyme or reason for it to happen. It can leap dollars in an instance, or tumble at the same speed. This means that if you do not have your nose to the grindstone constantly, you will be at risk of losing large amounts of money.

To stay on top and avoid feeling the sting of the volatility, you can join newsgroups on social media, download apps, and make friends within the game that will keep you alerted of the comings and goings. All it takes is one country to ban cryptocurrency, and the whole thing will collapse, losing all of your money in its path. For example, 36 hours after China imposed a ban on cryptocurrency, 75% of users saw dramatic reductions in their money. Keeping abreast of the news will allow you to make decisions after thinking about them, instead of making rash decisions when an event happens or directly after.

You want people to hold onto their digital commodities, however. That is how the market stabilizes. Be careful when you make friends that you aren't getting tricked by someone who is only looking out for himself or herself. Some people like to do the "sit and wait" game, and that has made some people quite a bit of money. However, many others get a thrill off of short selling or playing the market and making handfuls of money that way. It's all up to you and the way the market decides to shift.

Paying Taxes on Bitcoin Income

Bitcoins do come with tax implications and can be taxed by the federal, state, and local governments. There is a tax when you cash out your Bitcoins with any banking firm, or when you show dividends at the end of the year. Bitcoin is what many tax specialists would call an "asset." When you withhold any of your income that came from Bitcoin, you are actually committing a federal crime. Think of it as a bartering system, your Bitcoins are your goods, but they still have a monetary value that one cannot simply ignore.

It is best not to do your own taxes if you are frequently working with Bitcoins or you are working with a large amount of money. Do some searching online and find someone who specializes in working with Bitcoin operations. More and more tax firms are bringing in people who can help with that process so that you don't accidentally cause any problems between you and the state or you and the feds.

Of course this book is not a replacement for professional tax advice - please ask your accountant.

Getting Attacked by a Cyber Criminal

You probably are not the only person who finds the rise of the Bitcoin as something you can use to get yourself some money. The dramatic and highly publicized rise in the value of the Bitcoin has caught the attention of many cyber criminals. Why? There is an extremely low risk of getting caught. If you are not constantly vigilant and you make a bit of money, you will be at risk for hackers.

For example, one marketplace called The Sheep Marketplace had a totally of 96,000 Bitcoins that were worth nearly $220 million US dollars – quite a bit of change. In early 2013, all of that was stolen. Similarly, some cyber criminals attack smaller scale accounts because they are typically easier to hack and add up over time.

Criminals will most likely try targeting computers connected to the internet without a good firewall, and break into the wallets. They use phishing tactics, malware, social engineering, and other malicious tasks that will create quite a mess for you to clean up. In November of 2012, thieves stole a million dollars' worth of Bitcoins from a Denmark-based payment processor. The result was a lot of lost money and headaches for everyone involved.

But don't think those cyber hackers cannot get to you if they can't get to your account. That particular attack made the Bitcoin prices drop dramatically from 49.10 dollar all the way to 39.30 dollars in a matter of nine short hours. This happened because there was a fifteen-minute trade lag time, meaning that traders couldn't get access to the newest and latest market information. It created a blind spot that caused massive causalities and money lost.

Sometimes cyber attackers will start a train of happenings that will indirectly affect your for months at a time. Other times, they will simply target out your wallet, mining pool, or even your computer. Make sure you have all of the available security and you constantly keep your eyes on your funds and the rises and falls of the market.

Bitcoin is doing all they can in order to stop the attacks, but it isn't possible to reign everyone in. From hackers to men living in their parent's basements, everyone who wants to make a quick buck is going to try as hard as they can to make it a reality. Stay vigilant.

Psychology and Timing

While you can't track the rises and falls of the Bitcoin market quite like you can with the regular stock market, there are ways to use psychology to make educated guesses or hypotheses about what the market is going to do. It is best to make notes about the following when you are looking to do some trading.

Days of the Week: What days of the week see more movement? Make sure you mark it down – Fridays might be a little busier because people aren't paying as much attention at work, whereas Mondays will be a little slower because people are still quite groggy from the weekend and the start of the workweek.

Time of Day: Forgetting just the day, consider monitoring the time of day. Are people buying and selling more during the morning of the afternoon? What about after the workday ends? Lunch hour? By making note of these important times, you will be able to schedule yourself time to pay extra attention. You can use busier times to your advantage, but you can also definitely use those slower times as well. Don't take just a week as the gospel truth, instead monitor it over a few weeks.

Holidays: Are the markets faster or slower during the holidays? Typically from November through December, people are taking money out of Bitcoins in order to purchase presents and trips back to their hometowns. Pay special attention to the market during that time. Once the New Year starts up again, then more and more people will be coming back into the market. You should also consider paying attention during tax season, at the start of the summer, and in August and September for the start of the school year.

Events: Make sure you pay attention to daily events that can happen on Bitcoin. The Toyko based Mt. Gox went down for an hour in 2013 after the value of the currency rose 20%, this had a massive, massive impact on the relative value of the Bitcoin. Make sure to pay attention to things like weather events as well – if the entire East Coast of the United States is going to have an ice storm that will knock out power for a week or even just a few days, people are going to pull their money out, and quickly.

The way you track any of this information is up to you. You can make a legal pad full of notes that you follow, or you can track it in an Excel sheet. The important part is that you are constantly watching and making notes that you understand. Once again, this is where it would be a great idea to have a team of people working together to help each other out.

SUCCESS (AND CAUTIONARY) STORIES

If you are feeling hesitant about starting to buy and trade Bitcoins, here are just a few success stories to get you motivated.

Norway

A man named Kristoffer Koch decided, on a complete whim, that he was going to invest $150 kroner (which is about $26 dollars in the United States) in Bitcoin in 2009. That simple $26 (what many people spend on coffee in a typical week), lead to a return investment of $850,000 or roughly 158,978 cups of coffee. Koch did not know much about the currency, but was doing research for his thesis on encryption and decided to put a small investment into the Bitcoin out of curiosity. He had no idea what he did was give himself a sizeable nest egg for the future. What did he do next? He forgot about it.

He forgot about the $26 and continued on with his life, graduated college, got a job, and started a family. It was not until the media and his friends started discussing the Bitcoin attention that he even remembered that small amount of money. His curiosity piqued, he had to think long and hard about his password to his wallet. It took him a few months, but he figured it out.

"It said I had 5,000 bitcoins in there. Measuring that in today's rates it's about five million kroner," Koch told NRK, according to a Guardian translation. 5,000 Bitcoins is $850,000.

Had he waited until today, his initial investment, with the single Bitcoin being worth $210, would be worth approximately $1 million cold hard cash.

Koch isn't the only person who has benefitted from the rise in bitcoins' worth and popularity. According to an April report by Bloomberg Businessweek, the success of the world's first decentralized, peer-to-peer digital currency has spawned many overnight millionaires.

Younger Generations

But Bitcoin doesn't only belong to those who have a college education. A well-timed investment of $1,000 in gift money by a 15 year old boy from Idaho has allowed him to earn 110x that money ($110,000) and start his own education startup.

Erik Finman took $1,000 he received as an Easter gift from his grandmother and invested it in Bitcoin back in 2012, according to a report by Mashable. After holding steady in Bitcoin for over a year, Finman sold his bitcoins for $110,000 – making him one of the youngest success stories out there.
Luckily for Finman, he sold his stash of bitcoins when the price hovered around $1,200 per bitcoin.

Finman, in the long run, decided to reinvest his earnings into Botangle.com, an online video tutoring service that "allows students and tutors access to a diverse array of resources that just do not exist in a normal classroom setting," according to its official website. Most notably of his success and company, Finman pays his employees in Bitcoin. He told Mashable that he enjoys "sharing the wealth of bitcoin", saying:

"I have no doubt it will be huger [sic] than anyone can imagine right now. Bitcoin is like the Internet in the '90s."

During a question-and-answer session that he took part in after his success on an Entrepreneur subreddit, Finman explained how he first came to learn about bitcoin, writing:

"I owe a lot to my older brother. He told me about bitcoins and help[ed] me get set up with 0.2 bitcoins that he gave me. And my grandmother just out of the blue gave me a $1,000 check for Easter."

He continued by saying that he accrued more Bitcoins and planned on making even more, "So that I can trump my brother in how many bitcoins he had," adding that he first learned about Bitcoin in 2010.

Though entrepreneurs today may not be able to replicate Finman's success, or they may fear doing so due to the risks and busier market, they can learn from those who have entered the industry through more conventional in-roads.

Cautionary Tale

Finally, we have a cautionary tale to keep in mind when setting up your Bitcoin account.

A male Bitcoin trader tells his tale occasionally, never revealing his name or location. In May of 2011, he put in $75 into Bitcoin. He played around for a few weeks and then went through one of the biggest crashes in Bitcoin history. After that, he lost interest, thinking he would never be able to recoup his money.

He stopped playing and moved onto something else.

When Bitcoin introduced encryptable wallets, he set up an impenetrable password. That little bit got him interested again, and he started buying a selling again, sending money to that locked wallet. Once the prices started rising again, he wanted to take his money and run. Just one problem: he didn't remember that impenetrable password that he had set up.

What does he know? He knows that he wrote down the password in a notebook that is somewhere in his house – possible in a notebook with all of his school things that just so happens to be the attic. He does not remember his password, and he's not sure he'll think of it in time.

For now, he's hoping that he can find the notebook and unlock his wallet. He knows he's still earning money and has a nice little fun set up for him. Bitcoin cannot access his password either.

Make sure you know where you put your wallet password, or you will have a ton of (possibly inaccessible) money just sitting in cyberspace.

CONCLUSION

There is no doubt that investing in the Bitcoin can be profitable. There is also no doubt that investing in the Bitcoin can be extremely dangerous. This is not one of those "get rich quickly" schemes, and this is not a cheat to get out of working for your money. In fact, to make the money you would need to survive, you'd have to work really, really hard.

Weigh the pros and cons, and talk to people on message boards or in forums that can educate you on what they have gone through. There are a plethora of YouTube videos out there that will help you along your path, including interviews with successes and failures. Though it may seem like pretend because it is on the internet, Bitcoins can cost you real money.

The best advice to take is to start very small. Do not go all in unless you know what you are doing, you know how to play the game, and you know you will get money out at the other end, no matter how long it takes you to get there.

Still, you can't be too cautious. You are not going to get anywhere unless you start. It's much like learning how to use a new phone or how to drive a car, eventually you will get better at reading the signs and you'll know where to click, who to talk to, and what moves to make.

I sincerely hope the information contained will help you to understand the basics of the digital currency of the future: Bitcoins. In an ever-evolving global economy, it's easy to see the benefits of this crypto-currency, while also recognizing the possible pitfalls. The best idea is to keep yourself abreast of the information, and staying well-informed of the technology and logistics behind this game-changing digital currency of the future.

Finally, if you enjoyed this book, please click below to share your thoughts and post a positive review on Amazon. I would greatly appreciate your support!

Thank you and good luck!

Benjamin Tideas

For More Bitcoin Related Resources including a free refresher course, cryptocurrencies guide and more, please go to:

www.plaid-enterprises.com/bitcoin

© COPYRIGHT 2015 BY PLAID ENTERPRISES - ALL RIGHTS RESERVED.

This document is geared towards providing exact and reliable information in regards to the topic and issue covered. The publication is sold on the idea that the publisher is not required to render accounting, legal, or medically qualified services - officially permitted or otherwise. If advice is necessary, legal or professional, a practiced individual in the profession should be ordered.

From a Declaration of Principles which was accepted and approved equally by a Committee of the American Bar Association and a Committee of Publishers and Associations.

In no way is it legal to reproduce, duplicate, or transmit any part of this document by either electronic means or printed format. Recording of this publication is not allowed unless with written permission from the publisher. All rights are reserved.

The information provided herein is stated to be truthful and consistent, in that any liability, in terms of inattention or otherwise, by any usage or abuse of any policies, processes, or directions contained within is the solitary and utter responsibility of the recipient reader. Under no circumstances will any legal liability or blame be held by the publisher for any reparation, damages, or monetary loss due to the information within, either directly or indirectly.

Respective authors own all copyrights not held by the publisher.

The information within is offered for informational purposes solely and is universal as so. The presentation of the information is without a contract or any guarantee assurance.

The trademarks that are used are without any consent, and the publication of the trademark is without permission or backing by the trademark owner. All trademarks and brands within this book are for clarifying purposes only and are the property of the owners themselves, not affiliated with this document.